# THE CHRISTMAS SPIRIT

## *A* CELEBRATION *in* WORD *&* SONG

# THE CHRISTMAS SPIRIT

### A CELEBRATION
### in WORD & SONG

## GLENN DROMGOOLE

ISBN: 979-8-9988655-0-3

Published by Texas Star Trading Company
174 Cypress Street, Abilene, Texas 79601
www.TexasStarTrading.com
(325) 672-9696

Designed by Lauren Monsey, Monsey Creative LLC

Printed in the U.S.A.

# For Carol

"Joy to the World"
is my second favorite
Christmas carol.

You are my favorite!

You bring so much joy
to my world
every day.

# CONTENTS

# SONG LIST

## HYMNS

## SECULAR SONGS

# FOREWORD

*The Christmas Spirit* will help you experience the Christmas spirit.

Glenn Dromgoole thoughtfully pairs his hope-filled Christmas reflections of that most joyous season with familiar hymns and songs that give each remembrance – be it a personal memory, a family tale, a poem, haiku, or a gentle reminder and thoughtful reflection – a connection to the songs we grew up singing at Christmas.

He offers the reader a moment to pause and consider what it means to give of yourself, to enjoy the season, to love another, and to reflect on the Christmas spirit. And to express those feelings in song.

*Jay Moore*
*Abilene, Texas*

# INTRODUCTION

Once again, it's beginning to look a lot like Christmas.

We feel it. We believe it. We sing it.

Christmas is the most exciting time of the year. The most joyful time of the year. The most generous time. The busiest time. Perhaps the most stressful.

It is, of course, a religious holiday – the birth of Jesus Christ, the Messiah, the Savior. Advent. Shepherds. Wise Men. Christmas Eve candlelight services.

But it is also Santa Claus and presents and parties. Decorated trees. Stockings. Candy. Crazy sweaters. Maxed out credit cards. Cherished family time. Anguished family time. Delicious food. Pies. Cakes (even fruitcakes). Decorated cookies.

And much singing. Joy to the World. Silent Night. Deck the Halls. Jingle Bells.

Christmas calls us home. Christmas is for children – of all ages. Christmas finds us wanting the feeling to last forever.

In this small book, I've tried to celebrate The Christmas Spirit through a selection of spiritual and secular stories and reflections, and pair them up with familiar carols. I invite you to read and sing along and share the joy.

*Glenn Dromgoole*

*The best way to spread*
*Christmas cheer*
*is singing loud*
*for all to hear.*

*Buddy the Elf*

# Part 1:
# SINGING

# JOY TO THE WORLD

1. Joy to the world, the Lord is come! Let earth re - ceive her
2. Joy to the earth, the Sav - ior reigns! Let men their songs em -
3. He rules the world with truth and grace, And makes the na - tions

King; Let ev - 'ry heart pre - pare Him room, And
ploy, While fields and floods, rocks, hills and plains Re -
prove The glo - ries of His right - eous - ness, And

heav'n and na - ture sing, And heav'n and na - ture sing,
peat the sound - ing joy, Re - peat the sound - ing joy,
won - ders of His love, And won - ders of His love,

(1. And heav'n and na - ture sing, And heav'n

And heav'n, and heav'n, and na - ture sing.
Re - peat, re - peat, the sound - ing joy.
And won - ders, won - ders, of His love.

and na - ture sing,)

# CELEBRATING THE JOY

The most widely published Christmas hymn wasn't written as a Christmas song at all. It is based on these words from Psalm 98: 4-6 (RSV):

Make a joyful noise to the Lord, all the earth; break forth into joyous song and sing praises! Sing praises to the Lord with the lyre, with the lyre and the sound of melody! With trumpets and the sound of the horn make a joyful noise before the King, the Lord!

Isaac Watts, who wrote so many wonderful hymns that are still among the most endearing in churches today, penned the words to "Joy to the World" in 1719. More than a century later, his poem was set to the now familiar tune we know and love.

And while he didn't intend it as a song about Jesus's birth, but rather about His second coming, today we sing it with much gusto during Advent and often on Christmas eve. It is my own personal favorite Christmas hymn.

I wish we sang it throughout the year, not just at Christmas, because we should be celebrating the joy of our faith all the time.

The joy of Christmas, to be sure. But also the joy of grace. The joy of hope. The joy of love. The joy of fellowship. The joy of worship. The joy of being alive.

We need more joy in our lives, in our world. And we need to recognize the joy that is all around us, even when sometimes it may not feel like it.

There's a great line in Philip Gulley's novel, *Home to Harmony*: "There's a danger in thinking joy is a matter of location. If we can't find joy where we are, we probably won't find it anywhere."

So, "Joy to the World, the Lord is come… Repeat the sounding joy… And heaven and nature sing… He rules the world with truth and grace."

Sing it. Experience it. Live it. Right here. Right now.

*Glory to God in the highest,*
*and on earth peace,*
*good will toward men.*

*Luke 2:14*

# O COME, ALL YE FAITHFUL

1. O come, all ye faith - ful, joy - ful and tri - um - phant,
2. Sing, choirs of an - gels, sing in ex - ul - ta - tion,
3. Yea, Lord, we greet Thee, born this hap - py morn - ing,

O come ye, O come ye, to Beth - le - hem!
O sing, all ye bright hosts of heav'n a - bove!
Je - sus, to Thee be all glo - ry giv'n;

Come and be - hold Him, born the King of an - gels!
Glo - ry to God, all glo - ry in the high - est!
Word of the Fa - ther, now in flesh ap - pear - ing!

*Chorus*

O come, let us a - dore Him, O come, let us a - dore Him,

O come, let us a - dore Him, Christ the Lord!

# ALL ARE WELCOME HERE

The church is packed.

The organ booms out the tune.

We all stand to sing, "O Come, All Ye Faithful."

And, well, maybe some of us haven't really been all that faithful. Some of us haven't been there since last year when we sang it.

Maybe there should be a verse, "O Come, All Ye Lukewarm."

Let's say you're here every week, giving of your time, your money, your faithfulness. Why should you have to give up your regular seat so we can all sit together as a family of occasional church-goers? Are we really among the faithful we're singing about?

But, then, listen to the words, "O Come, All Ye Faithful," and we realize the hymn is intended to be inclusive, not exclusive. All are welcome here – whether we come once or twice a year or we're there every Sunday, whether we are actually as faithful as we claim to be throughout the week, or wish we were.

The hymn doesn't condemn. It doesn't judge. Rather, it inspires. It sets forth a vision, a goal, a purpose, something to strive for, something to celebrate. It calls on us to be joyful and triumphant. And faithful.

Maybe this will be the year that the words sink in and become life-changing.

And we all sing in exaltation, "Glory to God, all glory in the highest."

# O HOLY NIGHT!

1. O ho-ly night! the stars are bright-ly shin-ing, It is the
2. Led by the light of faith se-rene-ly beam-ing, With glow-ing
3. Tru-ly He taught us to love one an-oth-er; His law is

night of the dear Sav-ior's birth; Long lay the world in
hearts by His cra-dle we stand; So led by light of a
love and His gos-pel is peace; Chains shall He break, for the

sin and er-ror pin-ing, Till He ap-peared and the soul felt its
star sweet-ly gleam-ing, Here came the wise men from O-ri-ent
slave is our broth-er, And in His name all op-pres-sion shall

worth. A thrill of hope the wea-ry soul re-joic-es, For
land. The King of kings lay thus in low-ly man-ger, In
cease. Sweet hymns of joy in grate-ful cho-rus raise we, Let

yon - der breaks a new and glo - rious morn; Fall on your
all our tri - als born to be our Friend; He knows our
all with - in us praise His ho - ly name; Christ is the

knees, Oh, hear the an - gel voic - es! O
need, To our weak - ness is no stran - ger. Be -
Lord, Oh, praise his name for - ev - er! His

night di - vine, O night when Christ was
hold your King, be - fore Him low - ly
pow'r and glo - ry ev - er - more pro -

born! O night, O ho - ly night, O night di - vine!
bend! Be - hold your King, be - fore Him low - ly bend!
claim! His pow'r and glo - ry ev - er - more pro - claim!

# A THRILL OF HOPE!

The popular Christmas carol, "O Holy Night," was first performed in 1847 in France and was translated into English eight years later by a Unitarian abolitionist who felt the third verse spoke to the evils of slavery:

"Truly He taught us to love one another. His law is love and His gospel is peace. Chains shall He break for the slave is our brother, and in His name all oppression shall cease."

In 1906 it was the first song ever transmitted by radio, and it has been sung millions of times in churches all over the world and recorded by country, pop, and classical musicians.

During this season of Hope, maybe we can find hope as well in the words from the first verse of "O Holy Night," "A thrill of hope, the weary world rejoices."

A thrill of hope!

Isaiah: "But those who hope in the Lord will renew their strength. They will soar on wings like eagles; they will run and not grow weary; they will walk and not be faint."

A thrill of hope!

Tom Bodette ("We'll leave the light on for ya!"): "They say a person needs just three things to be truly happy in this world: someone to love, something to do, and something to hope for."

A thrill of hope!

Martin Luther King Jr.: "We must accept finite disappointment, but never lose infinite hope."

A thrill of hope!

From the Internet: There are more than 100 villages, towns, and cities in America with the name of Hope, including these four from Texas – New Hope Town, Hopewell, Hope, Good Hope.

A thrill of hope!

A favorite book: *Good Hope Road* by Lisa Wingate features a young woman who, in her small way, gives hope to a weary community devastated by a tornado.

A thrill of hope!

A poem:

*Jesus speaks to us of grace,*
*Of hope and joy and love and faith.*
*Our Savior, Teacher, Master, Friend –*
*"I will be with you 'til the end."*

A thrill of hope!

"A thrill of hope, the weary world rejoices. For yonder breaks a new and glorious morn!"

# ANGELS WE HAVE HEARD ON HIGH

1. An - gels we have heard on high, Sweet - ly sing - ing o'er the plains:
2. Shep - herds, why this ju - bi - lee? Why your joy - ous strains pro - long?
3. Come to Beth - le - hem, and see Him whose birth the an - gels sing;
4. See Him in a man - ger laid, Whom the choirs of an - gels praise;

And the moun - tains in re - ply, Ech - o - ing their joy - ous strains.
What the glad - some tid - ings be Which in - spire your heav'n - ly song?
Come, a - dore on bend - ed knee Christ the Lord, the new - born King.
Ma - ry, Jo - seph, lend your aid, While our hearts in love we raise?

**Chorus**

*Glo - - - ri - a in ex - cel - sis De - o!

Glo - - ri - a in ex - cel - sis De - o!

# A PSALM BY
# ANY OTHER NAME

*Scripture: Psalm 24*

Hello. We Psalms have to stick together. Particularly those of us who aren't all that famous.

Take my brother. He's not just Psalm 23 – he's The Twenty-Third Psalm.

Everybody knows him. Preachers quote him at funerals. People write whole books based on him. Children and dogs follow him everywhere.

"Why can't you be like your brother, No. 23?"

"Because I'm No. 24," I say. "I'm my own person, I mean, Psalm."

I may not be the most quoted, the most revered Psalm in the Bible, but I'm in there. Psalm 24 – or as I like to call myself, The Twenty-Fourth Psalm.

I do have a pretty good line in verse ten when I say, "The Lord of hosts, he is the King of glory."

Well, I like it. Especially at Christmas when great choirs sing, "Glo-oh-oh-oh-oh-oh Oh-oh-oh-oh-oh Oh-oh-oh-oh-oh-ria."

You don't have to be the greatest Psalm to have worth. God loves me for who I am and for what I can do, and he doesn't expect me to be someone else.

He made me The Twenty-Fourth Psalm, and that's good enough for me.

# DECK THE HALLS

1. Deck the halls with boughs of hol - ly,
2. See the blaz - ing Yule be - fore us, Fa - la - la - la - la, la - la - la - la.
3. Fast a - way the old year pass - es,

'Tis the sea - son to be jol - ly,
Strike the harp and join the cho - rus, Fa - la - la - la - la, la - la - la - la.
Hail the new year, lads and las - ses,

Don we now our gay ap - par - el,
Fol - low me in mer - ry mea - sure, Fa - la, Fa - la - la - la - la.
Sing we joy - ous, all to - geth - er,

Troll the an - cient Yule - tide car - ol,
While I tell of Yule - tide treas - ure, Fa - la - la - la - la, la - la - la - la.
Heed - less of the wind and weath - er,

# A TENDER MOMENT

It was a tender Christmas moment.

I was speaking to a senior adult group at a church. It was their Christmas potluck dinner, and they had loaded the table with lots of homemade goodies. I was happy to be asked to speak, if for no other reason than I could have all the pie I wanted. Oh, yeah, and the potato salad. Yum.

After we ate, we sang a few Christmas songs. Hymns mostly. But also a few secular tunes, including one of my favorites, "Deck the Halls."

You know it. Sing along with me:

*Deck the halls with boughs of holly*
*Fa-la-la-la-la la-la-la-la*
*'Tis the season to be jolly*
*Fa-la-la-la-la la-la-la-la*

*Don we now our gay apparel*
*Fa-la-la la-la-la la-la-la*
*Troll the ancient Yuletide carol*
*Fa-la-la-la-la la-la-la-la*

Well, what made that song so special that night was the fact that the church's pastor was named Don. His wife was Carol.

As we sang the song, when we came to "Don we now," Carol laughed and pointed at Don.

And then, at the end of the next line, "ancient Yuletide carol," Don laughed and pointed at Carol.

They obviously took great delight in singing that song.

And every time I sing it now, I think of them, laughing and celebrating each other.

I have no idea what I said that night, but I'll always remember how "Deck the Halls" helped make my Christmas a little brighter, then and every year since.

# PART 2:
# GIVING

# SILENT NIGHT

1. Si - lent night, ho - ly night, All is calm, all is bright
2. Si - lent night, ho - ly night, Shep - herds quake at the sight.
3. Si - lent night, ho - ly night, Son of God, love's pure light
4. Si - lent night, ho - ly night, Won - drous star, lend thy light;

Round yon vir - gin moth - er and child. Ho - ly Inf - ant, so ten - der and mild,
Glo - ries stream from heav - en a - far, Heav'n - ly hosts sing al - le - lu - ia;
Ra - diant beams from Thy ho - ly face, With the dawn of re - deem - ing grace,
With the an - gels let us sing, Al - le - lu - ia to our King;

Sleep in heav - en - ly peace, Sleep in heav - en - ly peace.
Christ the Sav - ior is born! Christ the Sav - ior is born!
Je - sus, Lord, at Thy birth, Je - sus, Lord, at Thy birth.
Christ the Sav - ior is born, Christ the Sav - ior is born.

# THE CANDLES
# WE CAN LIGHT

The Christmas Eve service closed with the congregation lighting candles.

It was most impressive, all the flickering candles illuminating the sanctuary.

Yet, only moments before, there had been darkness. Then just one candle. Then two. Then four. And so on, as each person turned and lit the candle of the next person.

One by one, the lights began to glow until finally all the candles were burning.

None of us had done very much, other than turn and light someone else's candle. But together, we had filled the room with light.

One by one, we can make a difference.

Most of us won't be known outside our own circle of acquaintances.

Most of us won't be able to leave huge endowments to our favorite universities.

Most of us won't be congressmen or presidents.

But each of us can count for something important.

Maybe all we do is light a candle in someone else's life, but that light, that life, proves to be an inspiration to thousands of others.

Maybe we start a food drive or blood drive where we work.

Maybe we make it a point to write a letter once a week to someone who might need support or encouragement.

Maybe we teach someone how to read.

Maybe we can be the person who is called when there has been a death in the church or neighborhood and they need someone to take a meal to the family.

Maybe we are willing to devote ourselves to one cause – just one – and really work at that enterprise.

Each of us has talent.

Each of us has time.

Each of us has some money.

Each of us can make a difference for good.

Imagine what kind of world it would be if we did.

*For it is in giving*
*that we receive.*

*Francis of Assisi*

# IT CAME UPON A MIDNIGHT CLEAR

1. It came up-on the mid-night clear, That glo-rious song of old,
2. Still thro' the clo-ven skies they come With peace-ful wings un-furled,
3. Yet with the woes of sin and strife The world has suf-fered long;

From an-gels bend-ing near the earth To touch their harps of gold:
And still their heav'n-ly mu-sic floats O'er all the wea-ry world;
Be-neath the an-gel-strain have rolled Two thou-sand years of wrong;

"Peace on the earth, good-will to men, From heav'n's all-gra-cious King;"
A-bove its sad and low-ly plains They bend on hov-'ring wing,
And men, at war with men, hear not The love-song which they bring:

The world in sol-emn still-ness lay To hear the an-gels sing.
And ev-er, o'er its Ba-bel sounds, The bless-ed an-gels sing.
O hush the noise, ye men of strife, And hear the an-gels sing.

# THE SPIRIT OF GIVING

Giving – honest, generous, unselfish, loving giving – is what makes Christmas come alive in our hearts.

Gifts are a significant part of the Christmas story, the Christmas season, the Christmas spirit. The Three Wise Men brought gifts to the Christ Child of gold, frankincense and myrrh. We express our love and appreciation to friends and relatives at this time of the year with gifts of various kinds.

But not all gifts are the material ones. At this most special season, let's not forget some priceless gifts of the spirit we can give to others – and to ourselves as well.

We can give the gift of forgiveness.

We can give the gift of praise.

We can give the gift of understanding.

We can give the gift of time.

We can give the gift of joy.

We can give the gift of patience.

We can give the gift of peace.

We can give the gift of hope.

We can give the gift of love.

These gifts we can give at Christmas and throughout the year. Gifts that are not expensive – but certainly are rich. Gifts that are ours to give – and to receive.

# THE 12 DAYS OF CHRISTMAS

*On the first day of Christmas, my true love gave to me:*
*A partridge in a pear tree.*
*On the second day of Christmas, my true love gave to me:*
*Two turtle doves, And a partridge in a pear tree.*
*On the third day of Christmas, my true love gave to me:*
*Three French hens, Two turtle doves, And a partridge in a pear tree.*
*On the fourth day of Christmas, my true love gave to me:*
*Four calling birds, Three French hens, Two turtle doves,*
*And a partridge in a pear tree.*
*On the fifth day of Christmas, my true love gave to me:*
*FIVE GOLDEN RINGS. Four calling birds, Three French hens,*
*Two turtle doves, And a partridge in a pear tree.*
*6th. Six geese a laying*
*7th. Seven swans a-swimming*
*8th. Eight maids-a-milking*
*9th. Nine ladies dancing*
*10th. Ten lords-a-leaping*
*11th. Eleven pipers piping*
*12th. Twelve drummers drumming*

# GIFTS WE TAKE FOR GRANTED

The Gift of Life – full of possibilities.

The Gift of Time – ours to use wisely.

The Gift of Laughter – the language of joy.

The Gift of Talent – little things we do well.

The Gift of Work – making a difference.

The Gift of Generosity – giving what we can.

The Gift of Kindness – in word and deed.

The Gift of Praise – opening our hearts.

The Gift of Peace – with ourselves and others.

The Gift of Forgiveness – given or received.

The Gift of Sacrifice – unselfishness in action.

The Gift of Gratitude – a thankful spirit.

The Gift of Faith – something to believe in.

The Gift of Hope – anticipating the future.

The Gift of Love – the greatest of them all.

# SANTA CLAUS IS COMING TO TOWN

*You better watch out, You better not cry,*
*Better not pout, I'm telling you why:*
*Santa Claus is comin' to town.*

*He's making a list and checking it twice,*
*Gonna find out who's naughty and nice.*
*Santa Claus is comin' to town.*

*He sees you when you're sleepin',*
*He knows when you're awake,*
*he knows if you've been bad or good,*
*So be good for goodness sake.*

*You better watch out, You better not cry,*
*Better not pout, I'm telling you why:*
*Santa Claus is comin' to town.*

# THE FIRST TIME
# I SAW SANTA

Can you remember the first time you saw Santa Claus? I do. Well, not the first time I looked at Santa or sat in Santa's lap or gazed into Santa's beard. I don't remember those.

But I do remember the first time I really saw Santa.

I'm not sure how old I was, probably six or seven, and I'm fairly sure at the time I didn't realize what I had seen. That would come later.

I do remember it was a Christmas Eve, and it was after dark. We were in a hurry to leave town and drive to my grandparents' farm house where there would be cousins to play with, good things to eat, and plenty of presents.

We usually didn't leave for their house until after noon on Christmas Eve, frequently not until after dark. That time it wasn't until after dark.

My dad had been working all day helping deliver baskets of food and toys to the needy families in our town. That day, as I remember it, all the deliveries had been made but one.

There was a house a couple of miles outside of town where a struggling young couple lived with their children – I'm not sure how many.

Dad said he would deliver the food and toys to that home before we headed out of town. We stopped outside the shack where the family lived. We waited in the car while dad went inside.

For some reason he decided to put on a Santa suit he had used earlier in the Christmas season – at the church Christmas program or as the town's Santa arriving on the fire truck. He was wearing the Santa suit as he stepped out of the car and started making his way to the shanty.

As he approached the house, the children – who no doubt had been told by their parents not to expect anything for Christmas that year – saw him coming.

They began to jump and shout for joy. Santa was at the doorstep. And he had presents for them. Santa had not forgotten.

"I told you he would come!" the oldest brother shrieked. "I told you he would come!"

That was the first time I saw Santa.

# PART 3:
# ENJOYING

# JINGLE BELLS

### (Chorus and First Verse)

*Jingle Bells, Jingle Bells, Jingle all the way*
*Oh what fun it is to ride in a one-horse open sleigh*
*Jingle bells, Jingle Bells, Jingle all the way*
*Oh what fun it is to ride in a one-horse open sleigh*

*Dashing through the snow in a one-horse open sleigh*
*O'er the hills we go, laughing all the way*
*Bells on Bobtails ring, making spirits bright*
*What fun it is to ride and sing a sleighing song tonight*

*Jingle Bells, Jingle Bells, Jingle all the way*
*Oh what fun it is to ride in a one-horse open sleigh*
*Jingle bells, Jingle Bells, Jingle all the way*
*Oh what fun it is to ride in a one-horse open sleigh*

# CHRISTMAS IN THE COUNTRY

Christmas memories are made of these:

The endless drive to grandmother's house.

Seeing the Christmas lights in small town after small town along the way.

Christmas carols playing softly on the car radio and wishing for some rock'n'roll.

Sleeping on the back seat and trying to convince my little brother to take the floorboard.

Asking for the hundredth time, "How many more miles?"

Finally, the feeling as the car turns off pavement onto the gravel country road.

Honking the horn as we come up the lane.

Being greeted enthusiastically by aunts and uncles and cousins.

The warm feeling of belonging.

The freedom of being in the country.

Hunting rabbits with a .410 shotgun.

Pretending to like the taste of fried jackrabbit.

Having to go to the outhouse in the middle of the night.

Saturday night baths in a washtub.

Peaceful, restful, but never boring, lazy days.

The adults setting off Roman candles while we kids light sparklers.

The smell of turkey cooking on Christmas morning.

Great country vegetables, especially cream peas.

All the cousins eating off card tables while the big folks get the dining table.

The day when you're not a kid anymore and get to join the adults.

Wondering why anyone would eat mincemeat pie when there are so many delicious desserts available.

Sleeping on a screened porch in the winter under several pounds of quilts.

Waking up to a cold house. Backing up to a wood stove.

Eating all the peppermint sticks you want.

Singing hymns around an out-of-tune piano.

Sitting in my grandfather's lap.

Staying up late to play dominoes or cards with a grandmother who loved competition and grandchildren, maybe in that order.

Spending hours working a jigsaw puzzle.

Walking a mile with my grandfather to get the mail.

Carrying buckets of rainwater from the cistern to the house.

Chopping wood and not being very good at it.

Feeding the chickens corn.

"Helping" grandfather milk the cows.

Watching grandmother churn butter.

Thinking that all the work around a farm was a lot like playing – when there are plenty of cousins around.

Eating divinity, and understanding how it got its name.

Wondering why the adults sort of giggled when they talked about drinking eggnog. Learning why.

Having fried quail for dinner one night during the holidays and liking that much better than jackrabbit.

Wishing the holidays would never end.

*Santa Claus has
the right idea —
visit people only
once a year.*

Victor Borge

# HERE WE COME A-CAROLING

### (The Wassail Song)

1. Here we come a-car-ol-ing, A-mong the leaves so green!
2. We are not dai-ly beg-gars, That go from door to door!
3. God bless the peo-ple of this house, And all their kin-folk too;

Here we come a-wand-'ring, So fair to be seen!
But we are friend-ly neigh-bours, Whom you have seen be-fore!
And an-y freind that's in your house to cel-e-brate with you.

**Chorus**

Love and joy come to you, And to you glad Christ-mas too, And God bless you and send you, A Hap-py New Year, And God send you a Hap-py New Year!

*As we celebrate this season of peace and love and joy, there is one issue that continues to divide us – as a nation, as families, even as husbands and wives. There doesn't seem to be a middle ground where compromise is possible. No, it's one extreme or the other. You either love fruitcake, or you hate fruitcake! At the risk of offending those on the other side, here is my take on the topic.*

# DON'T GIVE ME A FRUITCAKE FOR CHRISTMAS

Don't give me a fruitcake for Christmas this fall.
The last one you gave me I couldn't eat at all.

What are those green things and blue things and red?
Are they still alive, or dormant, or dead?

I knew I couldn't eat it, right from the start,
because of my liver – or kidney, or heart.

I didn't want to be seen as a jerk,
so I just boxed it up and took it to work.

No one would touch it and by the end of the day,
not even the ants would take it away.

I offered slices to my former best friends.
They haven't spoken a word to me since.

I fed it to the dogs and they turned up their noses
and busted the fence and trampled the roses.

I put it outside when they made such a fuss,
and I wasn't surprised when it started to rust.

I tried it as a prop to hold open the door.
It left a gooey spot on the hallway floor.

I put it on the end of a ten-foot pole,
and dropped it to the bottom of a ten-foot hole…

And poured in gasoline and threw in a torch.
But the next day there it was, right back on my porch.

I finally gave it to my Aunt Ida Mary.
(You probably noticed her obituary.)

We buried it with her… and three days later –
it showed up again in my refrigerator.

And there it has stayed for the rest of the year,
gobbling my pickles and guzzling my beer…

Inhaling the whipped cream and butterscotch custard,
the blackberry jelly and a new jar of mustard.

I'm stuck with it now, for worse, not for better.
That's why I'm transcribing this urgent letter.

I beg you: Don't give me a fruitcake this season.
I'll refuse to accept it. I don't need a reason.

# WE THREE KINGS

1. We three kings of O - ri - ent are, Bear - ing gifts we trav - erse a - far,
2. Born a King on Beth - le - hem plain, Gold I bring to crown Him a - gain,
3. Frank - in - cense to of - fer have I, In - cense owns a De - i - ty nigh;
4. Myrrh is mine; its bit - ter per - fume Breathes a life of gath - er - ing gloom;
5. Glo - rious now be - hold Him a - rise, King, and God, and sac - ri - fice;

Field and foun - tain, Moor and moun - tain, Fol - low - ing yon - der star.
King for - ev - er, Ceas - ing nev - er O - ver us all to reign.
Prayer and prais - ing All men rais - ing, Wor - ship Him, God on high.
Sor - row - ing, sigh - ing, Bleed - ing, dy - ing, Sealed in the stone - cold tomb.
Heav - en sings Al - le - lu - ia: Al - le - lu - ia the earth re - plies.

**Chorus**

O star of won - der, star of night, Star with roy - al beau - ty bright,

West - ward lead - ing, still pro - ceed - ing, Guide us to thy per - fect light. A - men.

# NO FRUITCAKE FOR MARY

One Sunday pastor Cliff quoted the first stanza of my poem, "Don't Give Me a Fruitcake for Christmas," in his sermon.

*Don't give me a fruitcake for Christmas this fall.*
*The last one you gave me I couldn't eat at all.*
*What are those green things and blue things and red?*
*Are they still alive, or dormant, or dead?*

But he then proceeded to skate on very thin theological ice by suggesting that there might have been more than three wise men, and they might have brought more than gold, frankincense and myrrh to Bethlehem. Why, maybe -- and here's where it gets a bit slippery theologically – maybe they might have even brought a fruitcake.

Well, I certainly couldn't let that go unchallenged! And so, continuing down that slippery theological slope, what might Mary have done if they HAD brought the Baby Jesus a fruitcake?

❧ She might have tried to feed it to the animals in the stable, if they would even eat it.

❧ She might have left it as a "gift" for the innkeeper who made her have her baby in the barn!

❧ She might have figured that surely the fruitcake wasn't from the wise men, but from Herod, as a sign of disrespect.

❧ She might have given it to the Little Drummer Boy so maybe he would quit banging on those awful drums when she was trying to get Baby Jesus to sleep.

❧ She might have done what the poet more than 2000 years later would suggest: "Put it on the end of a ten-foot pole and drop it to the bottom of a ten-foot hole."

❧ She might have thought, "I bet no preacher in his right mind will ever consider that the Wise Guys brought Jesus a fruitcake!"

❧ She might have told Joseph, "Maybe you can use this thing in your shop!" As a doorstop.

❧ She might have sent it home with her mother-in-law – and it's been with us ever since!

Well, so much for questionable theology. I just felt that we needed to clear the air on this controversial holiday subject.

*At Christmas,
all roads
lead home.*

*Marjorie Holmes*

# UP ON THE HOUSETOP

(First verse and chorus)

*Up on the housetop, reindeer pause*
*Out jumps good ol' Santa Claus*
*Down through the chimney with lots of toys*
*All for the little ones, Christmas joys*

*Ho, Ho, Ho! Who wouldn't go?*
*Ho, Ho, Ho! Who wouldn't go?*
*Up on the housetop, click, click, click,*
*Down through the chimney with good Saint Nick*

*Ho, Ho, Ho! Who wouldn't go?*
*Ho, Ho, Ho! Who wouldn't go?*
*Up on the housetop, click, click, click,*
*Down through the chimney with good Saint Nick*

*The iconic Christmas poem, "The Night Before Christmas," was first published anonymously in 1823 as "A Visit from St. Nicholas," later attributed to Clement Clark Moore. Over the years, there have been numerous spin-offs of the original verse, but as far as I know, this is the only one applied to plumbing.*

# THE PLUMBER'S NIGHT BEFORE CHRISTMAS

'Tis the night before Christmas, the plumber's here late,
trying to unclog our toilet, at double overtime rate.

The problems all started, as best we can tell,
when Aunt Nora went to the potty and stayed for a spell.

We knocked on the door, several times in fact,
but Nora wouldn't be disturbed, and that was that.

Then what to our innocent ears should explode
but the cries of Aunt Nora, still on the commode.

"Hey, something," she said, "is seriously wrong,
the water keeps rising, and it won't be too long…

"Until the pot overflows and we have quite a mess.
We must call the plumber," she had to confess.

So I called the plumber, the one we call Gator;
he said he could come, not sooner, but later.

He arrived in six hours, not in his Chevrolet,
but with eight reindeer pulling a really cool sleigh.

Instead of the carport, they landed on the roof,
and he hollered instructions to the reindeer on hoof.

"Whoa, Bucket and Reamer, stay, Faucet and Sink,
and Number One and Plunger, and Number Two and Stink."

Gator didn't have on his old jeans that night;
he was dressed all in red, trimmed crisply in white.

His backside wasn't showing as he bent down to work,
and took out his flashlight to look into the murk.

We were holding our breath when he went to his truck,
then he came back and offered a prayer of good luck.

He scratched his white head, then broke out in a smile.
"It's not a big problem," he said after a while.

"You have a small stoppage and that we can fix.
Apparently *someone* has flushed their toothpicks."

He reached in his pocket and pulled out a chain,
then began to stuff it down the clogged drain.

Before long we heard a rumble and a roar;
the potty was flowing, it was stopped up no more.

Then what to our wondering eyes should appear
but Santa in our fridge, pulling out a cold beer.

He took a long swig, said, "Thanks for the brew;
it's Christmas Eve folks, I'm not charging you."

He hitched up the reindeer; we were all in a hush.
"Merry Christmas," he called, "and to all a good flush!"

# O LITTLE TOWN OF BETHLEHEM

1. O lit-tle town of Beth-le-hem, How still we see thee lie!
2. For Christ is born of Mar - y, And gath-ered all a-bove,
3. How si - lent - ly, how si - lent - ly The won-drous gift is giv'n!
4. O ho - ly Child of Beth-le-hem! De-scend to us, we pray;

A - bove thy deep and dream - less sleep The si - lent stars go by.
While mor - tals sleep, the an - gels keep Their watch of won-d'ring love.
So God im - parts to hu - man hearts The bless - ings of His heav'n.
Cast out our sin, and en - ter in; Be born in us to - day.

Yet in thy dark streets shin - eth The ev - er - last - ing Light;
O morn - ing stars, to - geth - er, Pro - claim the ho - ly birth!
No ear may hear His com - ing, But in this world of sin,
We hear the heav'n - ly an - gels The great glad tid - ings tell;

The hopes and fears of all the years Are met in Thee to - night.
And prais - es sing to God the King, And peace to men on earth.
Where meek souls will re - ceive Him still The dear Christ en - ters in.
O come to us, a - bide with us, Our Lord Em - ma - nu - el. A - men.

*I wrote this one in honor of my adopted hometown of 40 years –*
*Abilene, Texas, home to Dyess Air Force Base, the Storybook Capital of America,*
*three universities, numerous churches, and generous people.*

# THE NIGHT BEFORE
# CHRISTMAS
# IN ABILENE

'Twas the night before Christmas, the streets of Abilene
Were deserted as usual, all was quiet and serene.

Christmas Eve services had already unfurled
With children and choirs singing "Joy to the World."

We had taken Communion, your family and mine,
Just grape juice, of course, no actual wine.

We got home around one and turned on the tree,
Everyone went to bed except my wife and me.

Soon the children were sleeping, so I and the wife
Cuddled up and were watching "It's a Wonderful Life."

When all of a sudden we heard such a clatter,
I grabbed my shotgun to see what was the matter.

It was up on the rooftop, that much I could tell,
Whatever had landed was louder than… well…

And what should I find when I looked up in dread
But a B-1 bomber and a fat man in red.

He had a fuzzy white beard, he might be an alien,
Or drank wine at Communion – an Episcopalian.

He had a sack on his back: It was full of good deeds,
He said as he pulled out a list he would read.

"Our local foundations," he read from the stoop,
"Have goodies to deliver to non-profit groups."

"Some folks think I'm Santa," the fat man proclaimed,
"But I'm just the messenger, due no credit by name.

"Our three universities, and our hospital too,
All would like a new building – and that we will do.

"The Paramount Theatre needs a little renovation,
And here's money for some more downtown innovation.

"United Way gets a fair share, and so does The Grace,
The Library a new branch, City Hall a fresh face.

"We invest in the Chamber," he took a brief pause,
"And the Zoo and the Nickel and every cultural cause.

"Texas Tech gets a grant – I'm certainly no fool –
We're investing in its Nursing and Pharmacy schools.

"The Storybook Capital of America, I know,
Needs a few more sculptures, which we're proud to bestow.

"There's still money left over," he said with a smile,
"For agency salaries, at least for a while."

He got back in the bomber and it took him away
To his home in the north – just where, I can't say.

But he shouted in glee as he roared off in flight:
"Merry Christmas, Abilene, and to all a good night!"

# ALL I WANT FOR CHRISTMAS IS MY TWO FRONT TEETH

(Chorus only)

*All I want for Christmas is my two front teeth*

*My two front teeth, see, my two front teeth*

*Gee, if I could only have my two front teeth*

*Then I could wish you Merry Christmas*

*All I want for Christmas is my two front teeth*

*My two front teeth, see, my two front teeth*

*Gee, if I could only have my two front teeth*

*Then I could wish you merry Christmas*

# CHRISTMAS IN TWO WORDS

Express joy.

Welcome silence.

Renew faith.

Sing carols.

Cherish memories.

Observe Advent.

Follow Jesus.

Try forgiving.

Accept forgiveness.

Give generously.

Attend church.

Light candles.

Celebrate life.

Promote peace.

Decorate tree.

Enjoy children.

Go home.

Have fun.

Indulge yourself.

Eat pie.

Decline fruitcake.

Open presents.

Give thanks.

Embrace family.

Take pictures.

Share stories.

Watch movies.

Write Santa.

*It is Christmas every time*
*you let God love others through you.*
*It is Christmas every time*
*you smile at your brother*
*and offer him your hand.*

*Mother Teresa*

# Part 4:
# LOVING

# THE FIRST NOEL

1. The first No - el, the an - gel did say, Was to cer - tain poor
2. They look - ed up and saw a star Shin - ing in the
3. And by the light of that same star The wise Men
4. This star drew nigh to the north - west, O'er Beth - le -

shep - herds in fields as they lay; In fields where they lay keep - ing
east, be - yond them far, And to the earth it gave
came from coun - try far; To seek for a King was their
hem it took its rest, And there it did both stop

their sheep, On a cold win - ter's night that was so deep.
great light, And so it con - tin - ued both day and night.
in - tent, And to fol - low the star wher - ev - er it went.
and stay, Right o - ver the place where Je - sus lay.

*Chorus*

No - el, No - el, No - el, No - el, Born is the King of Is - ra - el.

# A BOX OF OLD TOYS

It was Christmas Eve. I was at the office late, putting out the Christmas Day edition at the newspaper where I worked. Everyone else had gone, save one or two other souls who were printing the paper.

A woman appeared at the door, desperate. She had just driven back into town after spending the past week with her husband, who was out of work and was hospitalized in another city. She had spent her last dollar on gasoline to get home.

She had hoped to get back in time to pick up some toys for her two children from the Salvation Army or from the Christmas fund which our newspaper sponsored.

But here it was, late on Christmas Eve, and she had no toys, and no money.

Was there anything we could do?

Earlier in the week, our newspaper office had been overflowing with toys and food. We had sacks of fruit, canned goods and turkeys lined up in all the hallways and empty offices. By Christmas Eve, though, it was all gone. The food and toys had been distributed.

I could offer her little hope. She was too late. Even if she had come by just a few hours earlier, we might have had something. At the very least, we would have taken up a collection among ourselves.

But, I said, why don't we look around anyway.

We went into the big room where we had assembled the packages of food and toys. The room was a mess of empty boxes, wrappers and torn sacks. No one was going to clean it up on Christmas Eve.

Over in the corner we found a box of old, broken toys – too

damaged to be given as Christmas presents. Surely she didn't want those.

As we rummaged through the rubbish, however, we found a doll that with a little care could be as good as new.

And there was a ball no one had taken.

And how about this truck – it's not too bad.

Oh, she said, these will do just fine. I told her to take whatever she wanted. She picked out a few other toys which could be salvaged. In another corner of the room we found a case of apples and a crate of oranges which had somehow been overlooked.

By the time we were finished, we had loaded down the back of her old station wagon. It wasn't much, just some fruit and a few beat-up old toys.

But if you measure gifts by the size of the heart rather than the size of the purchase, I'll bet no one in town got more from Christmas that year than that woman's two children.

No one, that is, but me.

*Gratitude is one of
the greatest gifts
you can give to others
and, of course, to yourself.*

*Oprah Winfrey*

# HARK! THE HERALD ANGELS SING

1. Hark! The her - ald an - gels sing, "Glo - ry to the new - born King!
2. Mild, He lays His glo - ry by, Born that man no more may die;
3. Hail the heav'n - born Prince of Peace! Hail the Son of Right-eous-ness!

Peace on earth, and mer - cy mild God and sin - ners rec - on - ciled!"
Born to raise the sons of earth, Born to give them sec - ond birth.
Light and life to all He brings, Ris'n with heal - ing in His wings.

Joy - ful, all ye na - tions rise; Join the tri - umph of the skies;
Veiled in flesh the God - head see; Hail th'in - car - nate De - i - ty;
Christ, by high - est heav'n a - dored, Christ, the ev - er - last - ing Lord:

With th'an - gel - ic host pro - claim, "Christ is born in Beth - le - hem!"
Pleased as man with men to dwell, Je - sus, Our Im - man - u - el!
Come, De - sire of na - tions, come, Fix in us Thy hum - ble home;

With th'an - gel - ic host pro - claim, "Christ is born in Beth - le - hem!
Pleased as man with men to dwell, Je - sus, Our Im - man - u - el!
Come, De - sire of na - tions, come, Fix in us Thy hum - ble home.

# A FAMILY CHRISTMAS

He was a sullen, rebellious teenager, and he wasn't looking forward to Christmas.

You've seen him. You may have tried to live with him. You may have even been him.

Not much fun to be around, quite frankly.

But, still, he's part of the family, so you do your best. Not that he's making much of a contribution to anything. Not that you even expect him to.

Just get through the holidays as peacefully as possible.

They were having everyone over for Christmas dinner. That is, everyone on his mother's side. They would go to the city to celebrate – endure – Christmas with his father's side of the family in a couple of days.

First, Christmas dinner. His mom had baked a turkey and made plenty of dressing and gravy to go with it. Green beans. Carrots. Sweet potatoes. Pies. Omigosh, the pies. Well, she didn't bake the pies; her mother did. Grandma to him.

And Grandpa, what did he contribute? Something in a brown bag, which of course was off-limits to anyone underage. Which made it all that more appealing.

But that wasn't going to happen on Grandpa's watch. Adults only.

Still, the boy eyed the brown bag. Maybe when no one was looking…

Grandpa saw him, walked over to him, put his arm around him. "Let's go for a walk," he told the young man.

They walked in silence for maybe a quarter of a mile. Then Grandpa said, "When I was your age, I pretty much resented anyone saying 'When I was your age.'"

The boy smiled.

"My last Christmas at home," Grandpa went on, "I couldn't wait to get away from there. And pretty soon after that, I did."

"Where did you go?"

"Well, I joined the Army. And the next Christmas, I've never felt more alone in my life, stuck in a foreign country, trying not to get shot, hoping I wouldn't have to shoot anybody."

"Did you?"

"I've never told anyone this, but yeah, I did. We were on patrol, and I heard a noise, and I called out, 'Who goes there?' There was no response, but there was a rustling in the bush.

"Again, I called out, 'Who goes there?' Again, no response, but still a small noise from the bush.

"I took cover and called out a third time. Still no answer. But it was obvious that someone was there, someone who didn't speak English. I could hear him breathing.

"I turned and fired my rifle. The rustling noise stopped.

"I crept over to the bush – and found a dead dog our unit had adopted."

A tear ran down his cheek.

"To this day, when I think of Christmas, I remember that pitiful dog."

The boy reached over and took Grandpa's hand and pulled him into a hug.

"Let's go join the others," he said.

*Christmas isn't a season.*
*It's a feeling.*

*Edna Ferber*

# ANGELS FROM THE REALMS OF GLORY

1. An - gels from the realms of glo - ry, Wing your flight o'er all the earth;
2. Shep - herds in the field a - bid - ing, Watch - ing o'er your flocks by night,
3. Sage - es, leave your con - tem - pla - tions, Bright - er vi - sions beam a - far;
4. Saints be - fore the al - tar bend - ing, Watch - ing long in hope and fear,

Ye who sang cre - a - tion's sto - ry, Now pro - claim Mes - si - ah's birth:
God with us is now re - sid - ing, Yon - der shines the in - fant light:
Seek the great De - sire of Na - tions, Ye have seen His na - tal star:
Sud - den - ly the Lord, de - scend - ing; In His tem - ple shall ap - pear.

**Chorus**

Come and wor - ship, come and wor - ship, Wor - ship Christ, the new - born King.

# LOVE TRIUMPHS

What Christmas is about can be said in two words.

Love triumphs.

The story of Jesus, whose birth we celebrate, is about that very simple message.

Loving is better than hating.

Hate destroys. Love builds.

Hate divides. Love unites.

Hate produces enemies out of friends. Love produces friends out of enemies.

Hate arouses suspicion. Love offers forgiveness.

Jesus came to say, "There is a better way to live. You really don't understand what it is that God expects of you. Here, let me try to explain it to you."

Love your enemies.

Understand the spirit, not just the letter, of the law.

Forgive those who have done you wrong.

Don't judge other people's motives.

Show mercy in dealing with others.

Treat people the way you would like to be treated.

The essence of life, Jesus said, can be explained in one sentence: "Love God with all your heart and mind and soul, and love others as much as you love yourself."

It is a message so simple yet so difficult to put into practice. Most of the people in Jesus's own day didn't get it. Nor have most of us since.

The message has been so distorted over the years by apostles of wrath and judgment, of hellfire and damnation, that many people have either missed the central point of Christianity altogether or have turned their backs on it.

Yet, along the way, the vision that Jesus set forth has continued to set the standard for how we should live. For two thousand years his words and deeds, his teachings, have been the conscience of the world. They have breathed new life into dead spirits.

His message has persevered because of devoted believers and in spite of misguided ones. It has persevered because it is true.

Even in a world where so much evil, so much meanness, so much selfishness seems prevalent, we are constantly reminded by unselfish acts of kindness and love that the essence of living life to its fullest is to understand that simple message.

Love triumphs.

Especially at Christmas time – when we are more generous, more compassionate, more forgiving, more sentimental, more spiritual – we catch a glimpse of the great truth that can radically change our own lives, and the entire world.

Love triumphs.

*Blessed is the season*
*which engages the whole world*
*in a conspiracy of love.*

*Hamilton Wright Mabie*

# AWAY IN A MANGER

1. A - way in a man - ger, no crib for a bed, The lit - tle Lord
2. The cat - tle are low - ing, the Ba - by a - wakes, But lit - tle Lord
3. Be near me, Lord Je - sus, I ask Thee to stay Close by me for

Je - sus laid down His sweet head; The stars in the sky looked
Je - sus, no cry - ing He makes; I love Thee, Lord Je - sus! look
ev - er, and love me, I pray; Bless all the dear chil - dren in

down where He lay, The lit - tle Lord Je - sus, a - sleep on the hay.
down from the sky, And stay by my cra - dle till morn - ing is nigh.
Thy ten - der care, And fit us for heav - en to live with Thee there.

# A MOTHER'S LOVE

Put yourself in Mary's shoes, if you can.

Here she is, about to give birth in a barn in a strange town. At nine months pregnant, she had to ride a donkey an excruciating journey to even get here because of her soon-to-be husband's political affiliation.

And when she got here, they wouldn't even let her stay in the house. She had to go to the stinking barn. Really?

It figures, she must have thought. She's already had to endure the winks and whispers of her hometown when she turned up pregnant and claimed that God, not her fiancé Joseph, was the father. Yeah, right, Mary.

So, now, here she is having her precious baby boy in a barn. No obstetrician. Not even a midwife. And Joseph? Well, surely, he's freaking out.

And yet.

In her heart, she hoped.

In her heart, she believed.

In her heart, she loved.

She loved this boy she was about to give birth to, this boy Jesus who would literally change the world. In her lifetime. Or sometime.

A bunch of star-gazing shepherds showed up, not the religious or political establishment.

And angels – with harps and halos.

And then, these wise guys with stately camels and nicely wrapped gifts.

And she hugged the boy she loved and dreamed about what might be.

He might become a pretty decent carpenter like his dad.

He might astonish the rabbis with his spiritual depth.

He might turn water into wine.

He might inspire thousands with his insights.

He might be the new Messiah.

Or he might die on a cruel cross. And then he might come back to life three days later and leave behind a legacy that would endure for hundreds, for thousands, of years.

A legacy of hope, peace, joy, and love.

A mother's hope.

A mother's love.

A Savior's birth.

*Once in our world,*
*a stable had something in it*
*that was bigger*
*than our whole world.*

C.S. Lewis

# ONCE IN ROYAL DAVID'S CITY

1 Once in royal David's city stood a lowly cattle shed, where a mother laid her baby in a manger for his bed: Mary was that mother mild, Jesus Christ her little child.

2 He came down to earth from heaven who is God and Lord of all, and his shelter was a stable, and his cradle was a stall: with the poor and meek and lowly lived on earth, our Savior holy.

3 Jesus is our childhood's pattern, day by day like us he grew; he was little, weak, and helpless, tears and smiles like us he knew: and he feels for all our sadness, and he shares in all our gladness.

4 And our eyes at last shall see him, through his own redeeming love; for that child, so dear and gentle, is our Lord in heaven above: and he leads his children on to the place where he has gone.

# TO CAROL
# ON CHRISTMAS EVE

*In our more than twenty-five years of marriage, I have left a poem in my wife's stocking every Christmas, thanking her for the precious gift of her love. Here is one of them.*

Finally, it is Christmas Eve
And it is just the two of us
For a few quiet moments

I treasure our time together
Always, not just tonight
But especially tonight

On Christmas Eve
When maybe all is not calm
But all is bright because of you.

*(On the facing page is one of Carol's favorite carols.)*

*She was so busy
doing Christmas,
there wasn't time to
experience Christmas.*

*Lori Copeland*

# PART 5:
# REFLECTING

# GO, TELL IT ON THE MOUNTAIN

Go tell it on the moun-tain, O - ver the hills and ev - 'ry - where;

*Fine*

Go tell it on the moun-tain That Je - sus Christ is born!

1. While shep - herds kept their watch - ing O'er si - lent flocks by night,
2. The shep - herds feared and trem - bled When, lo, a - bove the earth
3. Down in a lone - ly man - ger The hum - ble Christ was born;

*D. C. al Fine*

Be - hold, thru - out the heav - ens There shone a ho - ly light.
Rang out the an - gel cho - rus That hailed our Sav - ior's birth.
And God sent us sal - va - tion That bless - ed Christ - mas morn.

# CHRISTMAS IN 17 SYLLABLES

*The Haiku is a poetry form consisting of just 17 syllables in three lines, 5-7-5 count, communicating a succinct message.*

The Christmas Spirit
is alive and well in hearts
full of hope, joy, love

# JESUS HAIKU

Joy to the world – Yes!
We celebrate Jesus' birth –
heaven, nature sing!

Born in a stable,
worshipped by shepherds and kings –
and children in robes.

"Love your enemies!"
Oh, Jesus, why'd you say that?
So, who can we hate?

"Feed my sheep," He said.
"Feed the hungry and the poor,"
He says to his church.

A positive faith:
isn't that what Jesus preached –
grace, love, joy, hope, life!

That amazing grace
isn't just a song we sing –
it's our salvation.

Theology summed up:
Jesus loves me, this I know;
Bible tells me so.

"Blessed are the poor."
So what would He say today
about the homeless?

"Follow me," He said,
not just when it's popular –
but when it is right.

God so loved the world
He sent his son to save it,
not to condemn it.

"What would Jesus do?" –
based on the book, *In His Steps* –
more than a bracelet

Two thousand plus years
and still nothing can compare
with the truths He taught.

# I HEARD THE BELLS ON CHRISTMAS DAY

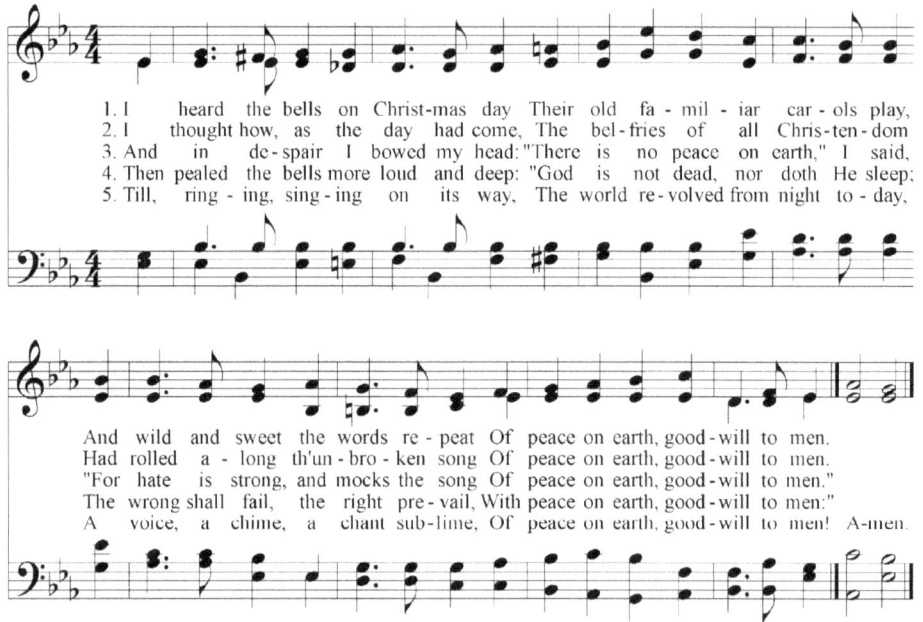

1. I heard the bells on Christ-mas day Their old fa - mil - iar car - ols play,
2. I thought how, as the day had come, The bel - fries of all Chris - ten - dom
3. And in de - spair I bowed my head: "There is no peace on earth," I said,
4. Then pealed the bells more loud and deep: "God is not dead, nor doth He sleep;
5. Till, ring - ing, sing - ing on its way, The world re - volved from night to - day,

And wild and sweet the words re - peat Of peace on earth, good - will to men.
Had rolled a - long th'un - bro - ken song Of peace on earth, good - will to men.
"For hate is strong, and mocks the song Of peace on earth, good - will to men."
The wrong shall fail, the right pre - vail, With peace on earth, good - will to men:"
A voice, a chime, a chant sub - lime, Of peace on earth, good - will to men! A-men.

# PRAYING FOR PEACE

More than ever before
I'm praying for peace
This Christmas season.

Peace in our fragile world
Where any day we could
Annihilate ourselves.

Peace in our divided nation –
For civility, for common sense,
For hope, for understanding, for good will.

Peace to those in power
Peace to those not in power
Peace to you and yours.

Peace in our families
Peace where we work
Peace where we worship.

Peace. Jesus is Lord.
Believing that with all my heart
And soul. Merry Christmas.

# WHAT CHILD IS THIS?

1. What Child is this, who, laid to rest, On Mary's lap is sleep-ing?
2. Why lies He in such mean es-tate Where ox and sheep are feed-ing?
3. So bring Him in-cense, gold and myrrh, Come, peas-ant, king, to own Him;

Whom an-gels greet with an-thems sweet, While shep-herds watch are keep-ing?
Good Christ-ian, fear; for sin-ners here The si-lent Word is plead-ing.
The King of kings sal-va-tion brings, Let lov-ing hearts en-throne Him.

**Chorus**

This, this is Christ the King, Whom shep-herds guard and an-gels sing:

Haste, haste, to bring Him laud, The Babe, the Son of Ma-ry.

# STABLE GIFTS FOR TODAY

Please join us at the stable, where we have come searching for meaning on this special day.

After the presents are opened, and the songs sung, and the dinner enjoyed, we look around to find the lasting gifts of today are not under the tree, but are here, in a simple and familiar stable:

The *love* of a parent.

The *life* of an infant.

The *promise* of an angel.

The *faith* of a shepherd.

The *generosity* of a wise man.

The *guidance* of a star.

The *peace* and *joy* and *hope* of a Christmas.

May these gifts be yours today and throughout the year.

# O COME, O COME, EMMANUEL

1. O come, O come, Em - man - u - el, And ran - som cap - tive
2. O come, Thou Day - spring, come and cheer Our spir - its by Thine
3. O come, O Wis - dom from on high, And or - der all things,
4. O come, De - sire of na - tions, bind All peo - ples in one

Is - ra - el, That mourns in lone - ly ex - ile here,
ad - vent here; Dis - perse the gloom - y clouds of night,
far and nigh; To us the path of knowl - edge show,
heart and mind; Bid en - vy, strife, and quar - rels cease;

**Chorus**

Un - til the Son of God ap - pear.
And death's dark shad - ows put to flight. Re - joice! Re - joice!
And cause us in her ways to go.
Fill the whole world with heav - en's peace.

Em - man - u - el shall come to Thee, O Is - ra - el.

# BEYOND THE MANGER

Christmas begins at the manger. It doesn't end there.

If we don't get beyond the manger, the wise men, the shepherds, the baby wrapped in swaddling clothes, we really miss the point of Christmas.

Christmas isn't so much about the miraculous way Jesus of Nazareth was born as it is about the way he lived. And the way he died.

We celebrate Christmas because of what Jesus taught, because of the example he gave, because of the new way of living he prescribed.

We celebrate Christmas because that little baby at the stable grew up to be a man whose life and death changed our understanding of God, our relationships with each other, our view of eternity.

Two thousand years later, we still find ourselves trying to measure up to the standards he set.

Love God.

Love your neighbor.

Go the second mile.

Turn the other cheek.

Don't be quick to judge others.

Feed the hungry.

That's what Christmas is all about — what Jesus taught about how to live a more productive and more abundant life.

If we could fully grasp the meaning of what he said and how he lived and why he died, we would indeed sing out on that most special day, "Joy to the World!"

And the next day, when Christmas is over, we would go about our lives with a different spirit. The true *Christ-mas* spirit.

# WE WISH YOU A MERRY CHRISTMAS

We wish you a Mer-ry Christ-mas, We wish you a Mer-ry Christ-mas, We

*Fine*

wish you a Mer-ry Christ-mas and a Hap-py New Year! Good ti-dings to

*D. C. al Fine*

you where-ev-er you are; Good ti-dings for Christ-mas and a Hap-py New Year!

# A BLESSING

May your days be filled with beauty,
Your hours with joy,
Your moments with peace,
And your life with grace.

# ABOUT THE MUSIC

## Hymns (in order of appearance)

"Joy to the World!" was written by Isaac Watts in 1719; music by George Frideric Handel, 1742; adapted by Lowell Mason, 1848.

"O Come, All Ye Faithful" – John Francis Wade, 1743; adapted by Frederick Oakeley, 1841.

"O Holy Night" – French carol, 1843, lyrics by Placide Clappeau, music by Adolphe Charles Adam; English version, John Sullivan Dwight, 1855.

"Angels We Have Heard on High" – Traditional French carol, 1842

"Silent Night" – Lyrics by Joseph Mohr, music by Franz Zaver Gruber, 1818.

"It Came Upon a Midnight Clear" – Lyrics by Edmund Sears, music by Richard Storrs Willis, 1849.

"We Three Kings" – John Henry Hopkins Jr., 1857.

"O Little Town of Bethlehem" – Text by John Phillips Brooks, music by Lewis Redner, 1868.

"The First Noel" – Traditional English Christmas Carol, 1823.

"Hark! The Herald Angels Sing" – Lyrics by Charles Wesley, 1739; music by Felix Mendelssohn, adapted by William H. Cummings, 1855.

"Angels from the Realms of Glory" – Lyrics by James Montgomery, 1816; music by Henry T. Smart.

"Away in a Manger" – Lyrics have sometimes been attributed to Martin Luther as "Luther's Cradle Hymn," but scholars have cast doubts on that. The first two verses are often attributed to "anonymous," the third verse to James Hamilton, 1895, and the music to James R. Murray, 1887.

"Once in Royal David's City" – Lyrics by Cecil Frances Alexander, 1848; music, John Gauntlett, 1849.

"Go, Tell It on the Mountain" is an African-American spiritual dating back to the 1800s.

"I Heard the Bells on Christmas Day" – Lyrics by Henry Wadsworth Longfellow, 1863; music, John Baptiste Calkin, 1872.

"What Child Is This?" – William Chatterton Dix, 1865; traditional English melody.

"O Come, O Come, Emmanuel" – Traditional Latin carol dating back to the eighth or ninth century; English translations by John Mason Neale, 1851; Henry Sloane Coffin, 1916; music arranged by Thomas Helmore, 1851.

## Secular songs (in order of appearance)

"Deck the Halls" – Lyrics by Thomas Oliphant, 1862; traditional Welsh melody.

"The Twelve Days of Christmas" – Traditional English Christmas carol and nursery rhyme.

"Santa Claus Is Coming to Town" – J. Fred Coots and Harmon Gillespie, 1934.

"Jingle Bells" – James Lloyd Pierpoint, 1857.

"Here We Go A-Caroling" (The Wassail Song) – Traditional English Christmas carol and New Year's song.

"Up on the Housetop" – Benjamin Hanby, 1864.

"All I Want for Christmas Is My Two Front Teeth" – Donald Yetter Gardner, 1944.

"We Wish You a Merry Christmas" – Traditional English Christmas carol.

*Sources: Come Let Us Adore Him: Stories Behind the Most Cherished Christmas Hymns by Robert J. Morgan; The Presbyterian Hymnal, 1990; Wikipedia.org, the Free Encyclopedia; PDhymns.com, a collection of Public Domain hymns; Hymnary.org, a comprehensive index of hymns and hymnals.*

# ABOUT THE AUTHOR

Glenn Dromgoole has written more than thirty books. He and his wife Carol own Texas Star Trading Company, a Texas book, gift, and gourmet shop in downtown Abilene.

Glenn was inducted into the Texas Literary Hall of Fame in 2019 and was named Abilene's Outstanding Citizen of the Year in 2013. He was editor of the *Abilene Reporter-News* from 1985-97 and co-chaired the West Texas Book Festival from 2001-2017. For eighteen years, he wrote a statewide syndicated newspaper column on Texas books and authors, and he is a regular contributor to the Spirit of Abilene website and KACU's West Texas Dispatch.

His book *What Dogs Teach Us* was a New York Times bestseller and won the Ben Franklin Award. More than twenty of his books are still in print, including *100 Great Things About Texas, Abilene Stories from Then to Now, Abilene A to Z, West Texas Stories, West Texas Christmas Stories, Coleman Springs USA, Just Happy to Be Here, Good Night Cowboy, Good Night Cowgirl, Good Night Little Texan, What Dogs Teach Us, What Cats Teach Us, What Horses Teach Us, A Few Encouraging Words,* and *Poetry for Men.*